A Magical Season

John Wheeler

Foreword by Hal Gambrel

Edited by Joe Land

Copyright © 2019 John Wheeler

All rights reserved.

ISBN: 9781702408707

WHAT SPECIAL OLYMPICS HAS DONE FOR ME

Special Olympics is a great organization that's done many good things in so many people's lives, including mine. If I wasn't in Special Olympics, I wouldn't be the player or person I am today!!

Before I joined Special Olympics, I played basketball for my school, Morristown, and I had a lot of good coaches like Tom Everheart. He coached me from 8th to 9th grade and he taught me a lot. He was someone who I really respected and trusted.

Then there was Craig Moore, who also coached me briefly when I played Junior Varsity for a couple of games—he was another coach I had a lot of respect for.

Unfortunately, during my Junior year of high school, I was cut from the team and that's when I found my way to Special Olympics.

A day after I got cut, a friend of mine came up to me and said that there was another team in Shelbyville that would love to have me play for them, so I decided to try out for them. That's when I joined Special Olympics and met my coach Hal Gambrel. That's when things got so much better for me because when I met Hal, my confidence in myself was low but he helped me believe in myself—this is a big reason of why I am the player and person I am today! Eleven years later, I've won six State Championships and had the most fun I've ever had in all my life. I am happy I decided to keep playing.

This is also why I encourage everyone who has a disability to join Special Olympics because it creates such a positive impact on people's lives. It made me a better person in so many ways, not just in sports, and it'll do the same for everyone that wants to join.

The coaches in Special Olympics are great because they truly care about their athletes and always do their best to help them get better and to succeed in life.

Special Olympics really saved my life—it's given me everything I could ask for, like good friends and great coaches who care about me and challenge me to keep getting better. The most important thing it has given me is another family—everyone in Special Olympics is considered to be family. I love all of the coaches and athletes and want to thank them for everything they have done for me.

The competition in Special Olympics is at a great level—about the same as a varsity high school game. When you look at teams like Warrick, Grant, Boone, Lake, and of course, Shelby, all these teams have great athletes and coaches who could compete with any team. That's why every off-season, I constantly push myself to get better because I know, all the teams I mentioned, every year they come back better than ever, which is why I have a lot of respect for them

Don't get me wrong, playing in Special Olympics is fun, but if you really want to compete, you have to put in the work, but I believe that the best reward in life is working hard at any work worth doing. If you have a disability, please join special Olympics—I promise it will do so many great things for you like it did for me.

FOREWORD
by Coach Hal Gambrel

The 2018-2019 season for the Shelby County Magic, an Indiana Special Olympics basketball team, was truly a magical and wondrous season. It was the kind of season that players and coaches are always hopeful for at the beginning of any season—a season when all things come together, the stars align and lightning is caught in a bottle.

First, some background information about Special Olympics. Special Olympics was founded by Eunice Kennedy Shriver in 1968. The purpose of Special Olympics is to give those with intellectual disabilities an opportunity to participate in athletic competition, so they may reap the rewards and benefits everyone gains from participating in sports. The lessons of teamwork, achievement, togetherness and the joys of setting goals and striving to achieve those goals, the "thrills of victory and the agonies of defeat" so to speak. This is accompanied by the opportunities to develop long lasting friendships with teammates and competitors, something that I believe everyone should have the chance to experience.

Indiana Special Olympics Basketball is one of the largest competitions the organization holds each year, it is Indiana after all, *the* state fueled by its passion for basketball.

One of the goals of Special Olympics is to have athletes participate with other athletes of similar ability. This is accomplished in Indiana Special Olympic basketball by setting up four divisions or levels. Level 4 is for the least skilled athletes and it goes up to Level 1 for the most skilled. At all levels the players are taught the fundamentals of the game, passing, rebounding, defense, offensive plays, and, of course, shooting. All levels are very competitive and a joy to watch.

At the end of each season Indiana Special Olympics has a State Basketball Tournament modeled after the Indiana State High School State Tournament to determine a State Champion at each level. The competition is quite intense.

The Shelby County Magic is a Level 1 team. The athletes on this team are the most skilled in the county. Several members of the team have participated in school sports with some success. Level 1 basketball is played and officiated by the same rules as Indiana High School Basketball. Most of the players are adult men. Most of the Magic players are in their 20s and early 30s.

Through the years our main core of players, since 2008, has been Calvin Hanna, Sam Gambrel, and John Wheeler (the author). Cody McQueary came along a couple of years later and completed a solid roster of players. Brendan Harris and John Buckel joined the team five years ago. Chris Vanarsdall, our youngest player, after two years of development on the Level 2 team, joined the team this past year along with Willard Sapp.

While the season was magical, it wasn't magical in the sense that something unexpected happened. A magician makes a trick or illusion by hours and hours of practice and hard work. This magical season was similarly produced by years of practice and hard work.

The beginning of this story started in 2008 when a gangly 16-year-old 6'7" high school boy, John Wheeler, showed up at practice one night wanting to know if he could play on our team. It didn't take me long to say yes. He wanted to play on his school team but didn't feel like it was working out for him.

The first year he was on the team, along with Calvin and Sam, we won our first State Championship at Level 2.

The magic of this team has always been their friendship, loyalty and love for each other, along with a strong competitive spirit. Oh, how they hate to lose!

They have an ability to focus and play their best in big games. Their belief in one another, as well as their willingness to take on any role necessary for victory, is an essential part of this team's culture. While many equate success in basketball to the number of points scored, the belief on this team is you don't need to score to have played a great game. Awesome rebounding, defense, passing and leadership all go into a great performance on the court. The fact that all eight of the players on this team buy in to this basketball philosophy is what sets this team apart from equally talented teams.

At no point in this magical season, even when we were behind or not playing well, did I look into the players' eyes and see panic or a belief that we would not win. Even when down six points with 30 seconds to go in a State semifinal game, the players were calm, cool and collected; they were ready to meet the challenge of the task at hand.

I can't express the joy of coaching this team along with the assistance of Joe Pugh and Joe Land. The fact that I had a courtside seat to participate in this season with the team through the highs and the lows will always be a most unforgettable memory.

The obtainment of such a lofty goal is a gratifying moment. This book chronicles the journey, for it's not only the sweetness of the final victory, but the journey that should be remembered and cherished. It is the hard work and sacrifice of the journey that makes the final victory so sweet.

Sit back and enjoy the ride of *A Magical Season*.

CHAPTER ONE
WHO THE MAGIC ARE

The Shelby County Magic is a traditional Level One Special Olympics Basketball Team who plays out of Shelbyville, Indiana and they represent Shelby County.

I just finished my 11th season with the Magic and in those 11 years the Magic have won 6 State Championships, 3 second place medals, and 2 third place medals. This season, the 2018-2019 season, was probably my favorite not just because of the championship, but because of how everyone on the team played with each other and got along with each other. As I said before I've played center with the Magic for 11 years now, but most of my teammates have also been playing on the Magic for a long time.

Like Cody McQueary, our point guard and my best friend, has been on the team for 7 years; Calvin Hanna, another one of our guards, has been on the team for 13 years. Sam Gambrel, one of our forwards and the son of our coach Hal Gambrel, has been on the team as long as Calvin has and is one of the best teammates I've ever had.

Brendan Harris and John Buckel just finished their 5th season with the Magic and both played a big part in helping the Magic win as many games as they did this season.

Then our two rookies, Chris Vanarsdall and Willard Sapp joined our team and both would play major roles in helping the Magic win a championship and making this season as great as it was.

Now we have our two coaches, assistant coach Joe Pugh and our head coach Hal Gambrel, both of them really helped me and my teammates realize just how good we really can be and why we were State Champions.

That's who we are and I hope by the time you've finished reading this story you'll realize why this team is special and why this was a magical season for us.

CHAPTER TWO
THE SEASON BEGINS

The month was December, a few weeks before Christmas when the Magic started their practices and when they came to practice that day, they had no idea what was going to happen for the season.

Most of our core guys were back from last year's team—like Brendan, Cody, Sam, Buckel, and of course me, but we also lost a lot of players from last year's team.

We lost Chuck and Brandon Horton, two of our forwards, Richie our backup center, Ryan Beard, our best three-point shooter, and Chris Thompson, one of our starting guards. They started their own team and competed well throughout the season.

Going into this season, we all knew a lot of people had to step up if we were going to win a championship. So when we started practicing we just scrimmaged with each other, tried to get everyone back in shape for the season, and to get our team chemistry back.

That's what we did for the first couple of weeks for practice—then, before Christmas came, we decided to put our offense and defense in place so we could get ready for our first game.

When our last practice before Christmas was over, our coach had a team meeting to talk about our schedule when we got back from Christmas break.

"Guy's you've worked really hard the past couple of weeks and I'm sure you guys will be ready to play when our season starts next month," said Coach Hal. "I hope you guys are ready to play because we're going to be tested early. Our first game is at Seymour on January 5th and if we win our first game we'll play another game, most likely against Warrick County!"

CHAPTER 3
OUR FIRST CHALLENGE

On January 5th of 2019 we all went to Seymour to get ready for their invitational tournament and while we were driving there, our coach could tell we were ready to play. When we got there we found out our first game would be against the Floyd County All-Stars, a team we figured we wouldn't have much trouble against.

We got to the locker room and we changed into our jerseys and then we went to the gym and started to warm up and stretch—and whatever else we had to do to get ready for our game.

When the buzzer sounded signaling the start of the game, we headed to our bench where our coach told us to play hard, come out strong, and to trust each other.

Then they introduced the starting lineup for each team. Our starting lineup was Cody, Brendan in our backcourt, and Calvin, Chris, and me in the frontcourt, with Sam, Buckel, and Willard on the bench. We headed to center court and we wished the other team good luck and we tipped off to get the game started.

We didn't get off to a good start after we tipped off. Cody scored on a layup, but after that we got stagnate and at the end of the first quarter we only had a two-point lead. When we went back to our bench coach Hal said "relax, attack the basket, play harder." Then the second quarter started and that's exactly what we did.

When we came out in the second quarter, we immediately did exactly what Hal told us to do and before we knew it, we had a 12-point lead going into halftime.

In the second half we were never seriously challenged and we let our bench players play most of the half so our main guys could rest up for the next game. the final score of the Clark County game was 47 – 24 and everyone played a great game, but we knew if we wanted to win the next game, we would have to play better.

CHAPTER 4
SHOWDOWN WITH WARRICK

After our first game, we stuck around to watch the Warrick and Porter County teams play each other so we could see how to defend against Warrick County.

When the game got to halftime, Warrick was up big so we decided to go out and get some lunch and talk about what we need to do to beat them. We went out and got some pizza, talked about Warrick but mostly we just had a good time with each other and our families while watching college basketball games.

After a couple hours we went back to the gym and started warming up for our next game and I could tell by looking at my teammates that we were ready to go. Then the buzzer sounded for the start of the game, so we went to our bench and Hal told us what to do.

He said "Close out on the three-point line, make them drive it in to John and Cody. Slow the pace down, control the temp, and don't turn the ball over, and play smart out there."

After he said all of that, Cody and I then told everyone to just play our game and to trust each other and if we did that we would have a good chance to win this game — we put our hands together and we yelled "Magic!"

We then went to the half court line to tipoff, but before we tipped off I looked into the stands and saw the McQueary's, Kendra (Cody's wife), and my aunt and cousin — when I saw them I instantly relaxed and was ready to play.

When we got to the tipoff, we wished Warrick County good luck and then we tipped off and the game began.

We won the tipoff so we set up our offense with me in the post and on our first possession I got the ball down low and I drove into the paint and scored to give us the lead.

On our next possession, after Warrick missed their shot, I got the ball again but the defense collapsed on me, so I passed it out to Cody who shot the three pointer and made it to give us a five-point lead. But then Warrick scored on their next possession to cut into our lead and for the rest of the quarter both teams' offense got into a rhythm and couldn't be stopped. By the end of the first quarter, we actually had the lead by 10 points because Cody hit 3 three-point shots and Willard and Chris both cut backdoor on Warrick and got two easy layups.

I also had a good quarter since I had six points and a few rebounds, but we all felt good about ourselves going into the second quarter when everything changed.

CHAPTER FIVE
WARRICK'S COMEBACK

When we got to our bench after the first quarter, Hal told us that we had played great that quarter and to keep it up and expect Warrick to make a run. When the second quarter started, sure enough we got off to a terrible start since Warrick changed their defense to a man-to-man, catching us off guard, and within a couple of minutes our 10-point lead was cut to only two.

So Hal called a timeout. "Relax, work the ball inside, and attack the basket. Don't settle for jump shots, be more aggressive," he said.

When we went back out on the court, after the timeout, we got together and Cody told us again:

"Relax and play together," he said. And that is exactly what we did.

When play resumed, Sam got the ball on the wing, he passed it to me down low and I got to the rim before a double team came and I scored. On our next possession, after Warrick missed on a three-point shot, Cody and I ran a pick and roll and Cody got to the rim and he scored to give us a six-point lead.

For the rest of the quarter, both teams' defenses dominated as we could only score two more points while Warrick would score four and we would go into halftime with a four-point lead.

During halftime we talked about how to attack Warrick's defense since they were playing so aggressive and physical, but we came up with a plan and felt good about our chances.

CHAPTER SIX
A NEW PLAN

When the second half started, we began attacking the basket on every play. I would get the ball on the high post and I would look for my teammates cutting to the basket. I would pass them the ball if they were open—if they weren't open I would attack my man one-on-one and try to get a good shot off.

It looked like our plan was working—I mean a couple times I got the ball, I found Cody and he made a couple of five-foot jumpers in the paint. Brendan also got involved on offense, one-on-one plays when I got double teamed, Brendan cut behind the defense and I got the ball to him and he scored on a layup.

Our defense was also great; we held Warrick to

eight points the entire quarter because we forced them to drive it in where Cody, Chris, and I were waiting—they couldn't score on us.

We also held them to one shot each possession. They didn't get any offensive rebounds and we challenged them every time they took a shot. Then the buzzer sounded signaling the end of the third quarter and I saw that we were up six points and I knew we had a good chance to win, but I also knew we had one more quarter to play.

CHAPTER SEVEN
WARRICK'S FINAL RALLY

When we got to our bench our coach told us to keep playing hard, keep pounding it inside to John, and to not let up. We still had one more quarter to play.

When we went back out on the court and we got ready to play—I looked at my teammates and I knew we could handle anything that Warrick threw at us.

The fourth quarter started and Warrick started hitting on all cylinders when they were on offense.

Within a couple of minutes our six-point lead was down to two. Then, halfway through the quarter, after we missed another shot, Warrick ran down the court and shot a three-pointer from the right wing, but fortunately for us, they missed.

Cody got the rebound and we set up our offense on our side of the court. I got the ball on the low post, but a double team came and I had to kick it back out to Calvin.

For the next minute Calvin, Cody, and Brendan ran the weave, trying to drain the clock, but Warrick was really pressuring them, trying to force them to make a mistake so they would get the ball back.

I ran up and set a screen on Cody's man and he got the ball when he cut to the basket and he scored on a layup giving us a four-point lead with a minute left.

Warrick came down with the ball and they put up a shot and missed, but Brendan fouled the shooter so they got to shoot two free–throws. They made the first free-throw, missed the second, leaving us a three-point lead with 15 seconds left.

I got the rebound and got the ball to Cody who dribbled down the left side of the court. He got double teamed so he passed it back to me in the middle. As soon as I got it, the Warrick County players started running toward me and I was about to call a timeout, but at the last second, Calvin got open.

CHAPTER EIGHT
SWEET VICTORY

As soon as I saw Calvin, I passed him the ball. As soon as he got it he was instantly fouled—he got to go to the free-throw line to shoot two shots.

He shot them and made both, giving us a five-point lead with under 10 seconds left to play and we knew that this game was over.

After Calvin made the free-throws, Warrick called a timeout to draw up a miracle play, but when we got to our bench Hal told us what to do. "Don't foul, just keep your hands up and your feet down," he said.

When the timeout was over, Warrick inbounded the ball and shot it from half-court, but it missed.

Chris grabbed the rebound and held the ball until the final buzzer sounded.

We hugged each other and looked up at the scoreboard and saw that the final score was 34 – 29. Cody led the way with sixteen points and I had fifteen, while a couple of others had two points.

We told Warrick "good game" and we got our ribbons. Cody got the trophy and we celebrated with our families who were there. We went back to the locker room and changed out of our uniforms. While we were changing, I told the guys that I was proud that they were my teammates because they always worked hard and never gave in when Warrick made a run.

They all thanked me for trusting them and being a good teammate. We all left the locker room and went back to the gym where everyone was waiting.

CHAPTER NINE
HERE COMES GRANT COUNTY

On February 2nd, almost one month after we defeated Warrick in the Seymour Tournament, we held our own tournament at Shelbyville High School called the Arnie Petre Tradition Tournament.

The "Arnie" tournament is one of the biggest tournaments for Special Olympics in Indiana since teams from all over the state come to play in it.

For the Magic, my team, we had two big games to get ready for. The first one was against our arch-rivals, Grant County. The second was against Howard County, a team we figured wouldn't be too much of a problem for us.

As we got ready for our game against Grant, I admit I was very nervous because we were playing our arch-rivals, on our court, and because most of my friends and family would be there watching.

Sure enough, when we went out to warm up, I looked up into the stands and saw all my friends and family there.

Seeing everyone made me feel better since I knew they were all there to support me and my teammates and I knew that we would need it today.

The buzzer sounded and it was time for the game to start. We went to our bench where coach Hal gave us some last minute instructions.

"Control the pace. Crash the boards, and don't turn the ball over," he said. We put our hands together and yelled "Magic!" and went to half-court to tip off.

When the game started, we got off to a slow start since our practice was cancelled earlier that week due to weather—everyone was a little rusty.

Grant County scored the first six points of the game and that's when I decided to be more aggressive for the rest of the quarter.

Every time I touched the ball, I attacked and scored almost every time. Grant County could not miss and by the time the first quarter ended, they scored seventeen points to our fifteen.

When the second quarter started, it was more of

the same—no matter what we did on defense, they still made a lot of their shots, but some of my teammates were starting to find their rhythm—like Cody getting to the rim a couple of times and making a couple of layups.

Calvin hit a three-pointer on our inbounds play to give us the lead for a brief time, but unfortunately, Grant County hit a three on their next possession to take the lead back.

Every time I touched the ball they would double team, forcing me to pass the ball to Sam, who would shoot and miss, but at least he was open—both times the ball just wouldn't go into the basket.

With ten seconds left in the quarter, we were down two points, so I got the ball on the top of the key and I drove it in and I passed it to Buckel, but Buckel didn't have a shot so he passed it to Brendan on the baseline. He shot the three-pointer but he missed and I got the rebound on the other side of the basket. I shot it and made it, but it was after the buzzer went off so it didn't count.

CHAPTER TEN
A WILD SECOND HALF

When we went to our bench at halftime, we felt good about ourselves since we were only down two points and we knew we could play better than we did in the first half.

When the second half started we came out firing, but unfortunately every time we had a chance to take the lead, we would make a mistake and Grant County would pull away again.

I was getting tired since I had to score the majority of the points in the first half, I didn't have much energy left in the second half—Grant County could tell I was tired.

Midway through the third quarter, I got the ball at

the three-point line. I shot, but it missed horribly and on the next possession I shot a 15-footer that also missed.

When the third quarter ended, we were down five points and we knew we were in trouble so I got the team together and told everyone to relax and that we were still in this game!

When the fourth quarter started, both teams missed on their first possessions. Grant came down and hit a three-pointer to increase their lead to eight points. With four minutes left, we knew we had to do something quickly if we were going to win. When we got the ball again, we pushed the ball down the court and got it to Calvin. Calvin got it and he shot a three from the baseline and made it a five-point game. On the next possession, after Grant scored again, we got the ball to Cody who shot a long three and he scored. It was now a four-point game with a couple of minutes left. After Grant missed their next shot, we got the ball to Calvin who made another three-pointer to make it a one-point game.

With a minute left, Grant County turned the ball over so we rushed down the court to try and score before they could set their defense up. Cody passed me the ball and when I shot, I was fouled.

I went to the free throw line, but I was so tired since I had played the entire game that I missed both free throws—Grant County got the rebound and we started to press them.

With fifteen seconds left we fouled them so they went to the free throw line to shoot two shots. They missed the first one but made the second, making it a two-point game.

We brought the ball down the court and Cody got the ball to me on the left wing. As soon as I caught the ball I was immediately double teamed so I passed it back to Cody who shot the three and he was fouled.

CHAPTER ELEVEN
A HEATBREAKING LOSS

After Cody got fouled, Grant County called a timeout to try and ice him. We went back to our bench where Hal told us to crash the glass hard in case Cody missed his free throws.

We went back on the court and Cody shot his free throws, but he missed two of the three so we were down one point with three seconds left on the clock.

We immediately went into a full court press with me covering the inbounds pass. When the Grant County player threw the ball inbounds, it went off my hand but it hit him again, so it was our ball. Hal called a timeout so we could set up a good play. I told him to let Cody inbound the ball and have Chris to set a screen for me on the low block. Hal told us to go for it.

We ran the play, but when I got the ball from Cody, I got hit from behind and lost control of the ball. Time expired before we could get it back. We lost 44-43 and our record went to 2-1 for the season.

After the game, all of our fans came down and told us it was alright and that they were proud of us for never giving up. That made us feel better.

After the Grant County game, we went to the gym on the other side of the school and got ready to play Howard County, a team we knew we could beat.

We ended up beating Howard 36-25. Cody and I didn't play the second half since we were up fifteen points at halftime, so we let Buckel, Sam, and Willard play most of the minutes.

After the Howard game, we stuck around to watch the Warrick vs Grant County game. Grant had the lead for most of the game, but Warrick came back in the fourth quarter and won.

Warrick, Grant, and us, the Shelby County Magic, were in a three-way tie for first place since all three teams were 3-1, but we knew that the season was just getting started.

After the game, my team and our friend Chris Thompson, who came and watched us play, went out to Pizza Hut to spend some more time with each other and to talk about the two big games the next day.

CHAPTER TWELVE
ON TO WABASH

The next day, February 3rd, my team went to play at Wabash College in the tournament they had going on there. When the season started, Hal didn't want to play in that tournament since it was the day after the Arnie tournament, but we convinced him we could handle it.

When we got there, we found out that our first opponent was Porter County, the team we saw play at Seymour against Warrick, so we weren't too worried about them. We also knew that if we beat Porter, there would be a good chance that we would play Boone County, a team we knew all too well.

The Boone County team had players who used to play for us, but they weren't able to make all of the practices and didn't mesh with our team. When we got to Wabash, we got there early enough to watch Boone play Montgomery County and we could tell that Boone was going to win and that we would be playing them after we played Porter.

Boone won by over twenty points and they also showed some weaknesses that we could exploit when we played them.

So after the Boone County game, we took the court and got ready for our game against Porter and during warmups I could tell we were still tired from yesterday.

When the game started, we settled for jump shots and three-pointers and we didn't hit any of them because we were still tired and sore from our two games the day before.

When the quarter ended we only led by two points at 8-6. When we got to our bench, after that first quarter, Hal said, "attack the paint, stop settling for jumpers."

When the second quarter started, that's exactly what we did—we attacked the paint and got layups, we pushed the ball, and forced Porter to run with us.

When the game reached halftime, we had a twelve-point lead so Hal decided to sit me and Cody for the third quarter and played us for a couple minutes in the fourth to make sure Porter didn't come back.

The final score was 46-35 and Chris played a great game which would carry over into the Boone County game when we needed it.

CHAPTER THIRTEEN
A GAME WITH OLD FRIENDS

After our game with Porter, we talked to the Boone County players—Horton, Chuck, Richie, and Chris. We wished each other good luck in the next game and caught up with them a little.

Then I went to get some lunch at the concession stand since we had an hour before our next game. When I got there, I saw my coach Hal so I got my bowl of soup and I sat down with him. He could tell something was bothering me.

"What's wrong, John," asked coach Hal.

"I'm still upset about yesterday, that I let the whole team down and I hope I don't make the same mistakes today," I said.

"John, forget about yesterday. You played a great game. Grant just hit a few tough shots. You just need to focus on today's game because we're going to need you," Hal said.

Hal got up and left, leaving me to think about what he said. I realized he was right—I needed to forget about Grant County and focus on Boone County because I was sure that Boone's coach, Kayla Thompson, would have a few surprises for me.

An hour later, I was back in the gym with my teammates getting warmed up. The buzzer sounded, so we went to our bench and got ready for the physical game to come.

We went to center court to tipoff—wishing Boone County good luck. We were ready to get the game started.

On the tipoff, I saw no one was covering Calvin who was in front of me so I gave him the signal and I tipped the ball to him and he got it. He scored on a layup to get the game started.

On our next possession, I saw Chris pressuring Cody at half court, so I set a screen on him and Cody got all the way to the rim. He scored and gave us a four –point lead.

Chris Thompson, from Boone, scored on their next two possessions to tie the game up. That's how the first quarter would go—with both teams scoring and retaking the lead.

For my team it was Cody and me doing the bulk of the scoring in the first quarter and for Boone it was Chris Thompson and their second guard Michael Grizzle who kept attacking on the baseline and scoring. When the second quarter started, we were all tied up at twelve points each, but then some of my other teammates started to get more involved. Chris Vanarsdall rebounded a shot I missed from the elbow and put it right back in to give us the lead again.

On our next possession, after Boone had tied the game up yet again, Calvin got the ball on the baseline and drove by Chuck; he scored and we grabbed the lead again with a minute left. Unfortunately, Boone County scored the next four points and they would take a two-point lead going into halftime.

CHAPTER FOURTEEN
A GRIND-IT-OUT HALF

During halftime everyone could tell we were tired, having played our fourth game in two days; all of us were sitting on the bench, drinking water, and trying to get ready to play one more half.

"I know you guys are tired, so when the next quarter starts, play slow, take your time on offense, but don't settle for jump shots. Try to attack the paint," Hal said during halftime.

The third quarter started and despite being exhausted we actually were playing really well, especially on defense—only giving up six points the entire quarter. On offense it was Cody and Chris Vanarsdall who carried us, since Chris Thompson from Boone was picking Cody up full court, I would set a screen on him and Cody would attack the basket.

If no one on Boone would stop Cody, he would get to the rim and score, but if Boone did slide over to stop Cody, then Chris Vanarsdall would get open and Cody would pass it to him for an easy score. When the third quarter ended, we were up by six points and feeling confident, but little did we know what was going to happen in the fourth quarter and what Boone County was going to try to do.

When the fourth quarter started, Boone County went on run after run to catch up to us, but every time they got within a possession, someone on our team would make a big play to keep us ahead.

Like when we had the ball with a two-point lead, I got the ball on the baseline and got double teamed by Horton and Chuck, but I saw Chris Vanarsdall wide open underneath the basket, so I passed it to him and he scored, giving us a four-point lead.

On Boone's next possession, Horton got the ball and he went up for a shot. He missed, but got fouled by Chris Vanarsdall so we went to the free-throw line and shot two foul shots. He missed the first one, but made the second, so we still had a three-point lead, but we knew we had to keep scoring if we were going to win this game.

After the free-throw, we got the ball down the

court and Cody got it to me on the elbow. As soon as I got it, Horton started coming at me, so I pump-faked him and got to the rim and scored. We now had a five-point lead with two minutes left. Kayla, the Boone County coach, called a timeout. We went to the bench and Hal told us not to let up because we still had two minutes left.

After the timeout, Boone County got the ball. Chris Thompson came down and shot a three with me covering him and he made it, cutting our lead down to two points with a minute and thirty seconds left to go.

After Brendan missed a shot on the elbow, Boone came down and scored again tying the score with less than a minute left in the game. We got the ball down the court. Me and Cody ran the pick and roll. After I set a screen on Chris Thompson, Cody got into the paint, but got cut off so he passed it back to me. I shot it but missed. Boone got the rebound and they ran the clock down to 10 seconds. Chris Thompson started to attack, but when he came down the left wing, the ball bounced off his leg and went out of bounds as time expired. We were going into overtime.

CHAPTER FIFTEEN
OVERTIME VICTORY

Four minutes. As we sat on the bench getting ready to play overtime, I told my teammates to play hard for four more minutes—we could win this game.

We started overtime with the score tied at thirty-five. When we got to tip-off, I thought about tipping it to Calvin but this time he was covered. I tipped it off to Chris Vanarsdall who got the ball to Cody and overtime began. On our first possession, Cody got the ball to me in the post and I immediately attacked the basket and scored, giving us the lead. On Boone County's first possession, Brendan committed a reach foul on Chris Thompson; this was bad news because they reached the double bonus and got to shoot two free-throws. Even worse was that Brendan fouled out so we lost our best defender. Sam came in and Chris Thompson made both free throws, tying the game.

Now the score was tied at thirty-seven with three minutes to play. On our next possession, I got the ball again on the elbow and I saw Chris Vanarsdall wide open again down low.

I passed it to him and he scored, giving us the lead again. Then Boone came down and Chris Thompson hit a three over Sam to give them the lead, 40-39, with a minute and a half left to play.

On our next possession I got the ball on the left baseline with Horton on my back. When I looked left at the paint, I saw Grizzle coming so I spun right around Horton and scored on a reverse layup. We retook the lead with a minute left. On Boone's next possession, Grizzle cut baseline again, but this time I was ready. I cut him off and blocked his shot. I grabbed the ball and saw Calvin running down the court. I threw it as far as I could and Calvin got it and scored, giving us a three-point lead.

There was twenty seconds left in the game so Chris Thompson passed the ball to Horton who shot a three, but he missed. Chris Vanarsdall got the rebound and then he passed it to Calvin. Chris Thompson tied Calvin up and a jump ball was called.

For some reason the refs said it was our ball with ten seconds left to play in the game.

Chris Vanarsdall inbounded the ball to Cody who passed it to Sam at the free throw line. I cut along the baseline and Sam passed it to me. When I got the ball, I shot it and got fouled by Horton. I went to the free throw line to shoot two shots—I made them both, making the score 45-40 with seven seconds left to play. After I made the foul shots, Boone called a timeout.

When we got to our bench, Hal told us, "Don't foul, just stay down and get the rebound when they miss." We went back to the court knowing we were about to win.

Sure enough, Chris Thompson got the ball and shot a half-court prayer that missed terribly. I got the rebound and held it until the buzzer sounded and that was it, we won and improved to 5-1 on the season.

CHAPTER SIXTEEN
THE MAGIC CELEBRATE

After the game we told Boone County good game, but you could tell they were upset, but they said good game to us too.

Afterwards we went to get our ribbons and the trophy. We got to the ceremony where they passed out our ribbons and I got to keep the trophy.

We stuck around for team pics and to talk to our fans who were there supporting us.

We went home and when I got home, I showed my mom the trophy and I went to my friend's house, the Langkabels to watch the Superbowl.

While I was there I started to realize that maybe, just maybe, despite losing so many players from last year's team, we could still win the championship, but little did I know what was going to happen next.

CHAPTER SEVENTEEN
THE INJURY BUG HITS

Our next two games against Franklin County and Marion County were complete blowouts as we won both of the games with the scores being 50-22 against Franklin and 47-28 against Marion.

In those two games, Cody and I played very little and our backups got the majority of the minutes to increase their confidence and to give the starters a break.

A week later during practice, Hal told us that Sam had an ankle injury and he would be out for a couple of weeks. Then during practice, Cody's back started hurting, so he had to sit for the rest of the practice. Later in the week, Cody went to the doctor to get himself checked out and found that he'd strained something in his lower back and would be out for a few games.

Another week later, on February 25th, my team went to Warren Central High School to take on the unified team there who were called the Warren Central Gold team. When we got there, we learned that Chris Vanarsdall wouldn't be playing that day since he had to work. We were down to five players—Calvin, Brendan, Buckle, Willard, and me.

After we got our uniforms, we headed to the court and when I saw the other team, I knew that this was going to be a very tough game for us to win.

The Warren Central Team didn't have much size, but they had a lot of young players, so they could sub in their players to keep them fresh while me and my teammates had to play the entire game with no breaks.

After we were done warming up, we headed to our bench where I said to the guys, "Alright guys, we're gonna have to play hard and smart if we want to win this game!"

I went on to say "There's only five of us, so slow the tempo down, take our time on offense and work hard on defense." We put our hands together, yelled Magic! and went to half court to start the game.

CHAPTER EIGHTTEEN
A GAME OF SURVIVAL

When the game started, the Warren team won the tip-off and scored on their first possession giving them the lead to start the game. We came down and got our offense set up.

Warren was in a man-to-man defense so Hal told us to spread out and attack the paint. Brendan passed it to me in the post and when his man came down to double me, he cut to the basket. I passed it to him and he scored, tying up the game.

During the next few possessions both teams would score with neither team gaining an advantage. When they had the ball, all five of their players would crash the glass and we weren't boxing out well so they got a lot of offensive rebounds and they kept scoring off the rebounds.

When we had the ball, Warren had no answer for me. I would score almost every time I got the ball. If a double team came, my teammates would cut and I would pass it to them—they'd score each time.

When the first quarter was up, we were ahead by four points, 16-12, but Hal was not happy. When we got to the bench he said, "You guys aren't working hard on defense. Close out on their shooters and box out."

When the second quarter started, we played much harder than we did in the first quarter. We kicked up our intensity on defense, putting more pressure on them and getting a few steals.

I got one steal when they tried to pass it in the lane—I took it the other way and scored. Brendan got a couple too and so did Willard. We also changed our defense from a 1-3-1 to a 2-3 zone. When we did, it really confused the Warren team since they couldn't figure out how to attack it. That helped us to pull away so when the second quarter ended, we were leading by 12 points, 28-16. We only gave up four points the entire quarter. Hal was much happier than he was at the end of the first quarter.

Going into the second half, we started to pull away, more as the third quarter went on. On defense, we stuck with the 2-3 zone and the Warren team continued to struggle with it.

On offense, I moved to the outside and took my man one-on-one. I figured out that my man bit on pump-fakes, so every time I got the ball on the outside, I would pump-fake him and then drive past him to get to the rim.

If the defense didn't collapse on me, I would score. If they did collapse in, I would pass it out to Calvin or Willard and they would shoot the three and they'd make it more times than not.

At the end of the third quarter, we were up eighteen points, but you could tell everyone on my team was tired—as soon as we got to the bench, we all sat down and started drinking water.

Hal could tell we were tired so he said, "Just grind it out guys, hang in there for one more quarter."

The fourth quarter started and up eighteen, we felt we could close out this game.

Two minutes in, our lead was cut in half since the Warren team hit 3 three-pointers to start the quarter. I continued to have to be aggressive on offense.

Again and again, I would pump-fake my defenders and I kept scoring.

On one possession, after Warren made another three to cut our lead to only six points, I got the ball on the top of the key and saw no one coming out to guard me. I shot it. Fortunately, it went in and when it did you could see Warren's spirit fade away since we were now up nine points with a minute and a half left to go in the game.

We wouldn't give up another basket for the rest of the game. They started to foul us so we extended our lead as every time they fouled us, we shot free throws.

The final score would be 46-35. I finished with twenty-three points and I scored all ten of our points in the fourth quarter.

When the game was over, Hal said to us, "good job guys, way to hang in there in the fourth quarter. Now let's go home."

When I got home later that night, I went straight to bed exhausted, but our next game would be much tougher.

Photographs

Shooting hoops with my baby brother, David, when I was about 7 years old at my grandparent's house in Morristown.

Me and my 8th grade coach, Tom Everheart, one of the greatest coaches I ever had. I am holding the most improved player award for the season.

The Magic about to receive their Level 1 State Championship (2019) Gold Medal. Willard Sapp, John Buckel, Sam Gambrel, Chris Vanarsdall, Cody McQueary, John Wheeler, Brendan Harris, and Calvin Hanna.

John Wheeler and Shelby County Magic Coach Hal Gambrel.

A big thanks to my friends that helped us at our final practice before the State Tournament. Zach Kuhn, John Wheeler, Dylan Pugh, John Buckel, and Max Pugh

The day that Hayden Langkabel (November 2017) signed with Marion University. He and his family have supported me during my time with the Magic and in Morristown.

Level 1 State Champions (2018), the Colts, in flag football. We are coached by my friend Joe Pugh.

2018 Track and Field Medals. I received the bronze medal for finishing third place in the 800 meter run.

CHAPTER NINETEEN
A REMATCH WITH GRANT

Five days later, my team drove up north to Taylor University to play our arch-rivals, Grant County, for a second time.

Unfortunately, both Sam and Cody were out with injuries, but we did have Chris Vanarsdall for this game. We figured that we would at least be able to compete with Grant. This game was important to me, not just because we were playing Grant, but also because my brother and my dad were coming, so I wanted to win for them.

Without Cody or Sam, I didn't know how we could beat Grant on their home court with very little fan support because we were two hours away from home.

I knew me and my teammates weren't going to

give up and that we would play our hardest. If we did that and played smart, we would have a good chance to win. With Cody and Sam out, Willard got the start with Buckel coming off the bench. Willard got off to a great start as soon as the game started.

On our first possession, Calvin passed the ball to Willard on the left wing and he shot the three and made it, giving us a three-point lead to start the game.

As the first quarter went on, we started to pull away. For some reason Grant didn't play with much energy. They made mistake after mistake and we took advantage of it.

Chris and I completely destroyed Grant on the inside. Posting up on them and for some reason they didn't double team us, which proved to be a very costly mistake for Grant.

By the end of the first quarter, we had a ten-point lead, 17-7 and I scored ten of those points. I had a great start to the game and more importantly, we all believed we could win.

CHAPTER TWENTY
PULLING AWAY

When the second quarter started, we continued to go right at Grant, attacking them again and again in the paint. We didn't settle for jump shots and we forced Grant to defend all five of us.

Personally, I couldn't be stopped. I scored or assisted on nearly every basked. On one of our possessions, I got the ball and drove it in the lane. When I went up to shoot, I got bumped but still got the shot off and scored. On the next possession, I scored and got fouled, I shot one free-throw, but missed. Luckily, Brendan got the rebound and passed it back to me; I took one step backwards to get behind the three-point line and I shot it and made it to extend our lead.

As the quarter went on, Grant County became more and more desperate. They started shooting contested threes that didn't go in. They tried stealing the ball from me, but never could. They also started complaining to the refs, claiming we were fouling them, but the refs shook their heads and the game would continue on.

With ten seconds left in the quarter, I got the ball at the top of the key and I drove it in. I got double teamed, so I passed it to Buckel and then he passed it to Calvin who shot the three but missed, ending the half.

We still had a twelve-point lead going into halftime so we felt pretty good about ourselves. Hal reminded us to not let up and that there was still a long way to go.

Going into the second half, we continued to play well, especially on defense. Chris was dominating on the boards, grabbing rebound after rebound, limiting Grant to one shot each possession.

Brendan, Buckel, and Willard were putting pressure on Grant's ball handlers, forcing them to commit a lot of turnovers and kept us ahead.

I was also having a good game. On one possession, on defense, I stole the ball when Grant tried to inbound. I took it all the way and scored. Also on offense, when I got the ball on the top of the key, two Grant players came at me, so I passed it to Chris who was wide open on the baseline and he scored.

Toward the end of the third quarter, Calvin shot a three and missed, but Brendan got the ball back, midair, and shot it one handed—somehow it banked off the backboard and it went in!

When that shot went in, everyone on the team started laughing because it was such a horrible shot and yet it still went in, giving us a sixteen-point lead going into the final quarter.

CHAPTER TWENTY-ONE
SWEET VICTORY

Going into the fourth quarter with a sixteen-point lead, we began to relax, which was a big mistake because Grant came at us hard as soon as the quarter started. Within two minutes, Grant cut our lead in half so what was a sixteen-point lead was now eight. Hal called a timeout to calm us down.

"I know you guys are tired, but there is still four minutes left. Finish hard, keep playing hard," Hal said.

We went back out there and did exactly that. Grant got within six points on three different occasions within that four minutes. Every time they did, we answered back with a few big plays of our own to pull away.

The first time they got within six points, I got the ball at the elbow and I pump-faked the guy guarding me. I drove past him and made the layup. A couple minutes later, there was a minute and a half left in the game. They got within six points again, so we made another big play.

Calvin and I ran a pick and roll so Calvin drove it in and shot it. He missed, but I got the rebound and immediately got double teamed. Brendan cut to the basket, so I passed it to him and he scored.

With thirty seconds left, once again Grant cut our lead to only six. They were trapping us full court to try and get the ball back.

Brendan got the ball to me and I got it past half court to the top of the key where I got double teamed. I passed it to Calvin who was wide open on the baseline. He shot it and fortunately for us, he made it, giving us a nine-point lead with fifteen seconds left. We knew we had won the game.

The final score was 40-31, giving us our revenge on them and we improved to 9-1 on the season. We were on a seven game winning streak.

After the game I introduced my dad, my brother, and my dad's friend Keith to my coach and teammates. Everyone seemed to like them, so I was happy.

We all went out to eat and we enjoyed the spoils of victory. After I got back to Shelbyville, I went and saw Morristown, my home town high school team, win the sectional title against Hauser. Life was good for me that day.

CHAPTER TWENTY-TWO
ANOTHER CHALLENGING GAME

After beating Grant on their home court while we were shorthanded, our confidence was at an all-time high. We felt like we could take on any team and beat them.

Four days after beating Grant, we had another game in Indianapolis against a Unified team called the Marion County Thunder. When we got there Hal told us that Sam would play a little, but Cody was still out. Chris had to work so we would only have six players for this game.

But still having just beat Grant without a lot of players, we were confident that we could win this game no matter who the other team was. When we changed into our uniforms and got out on the court for warm-ups, I saw the other team and knew we were going to have to work hard to win.

The Marion County team had three guys who were at least 6'3" and they also had a very talented point guard. I was sure they could score a lot of points.

When the game started, both teams' offense couldn't be stopped. We scored the game's first eight points, but then Marion came back to tie the game.

Calvin picked up where he left off against Grant. He hit a three and scored on a layup giving him five points in the first quarter.

Marion County's offense was just explosive. Their point guard kept penetrating our 1-3-1 zone and he kept scoring. When he missed, their big guys would get the rebound and score.

Hal told us for the rest of the game we were going to play a 3-2 zone, something we had been practicing the past couple of weeks to get ready for state. That's what we did when the second quarter started and it worked against their point guard. He started to get frustrated but we still had trouble with their big guys. Fortunately, I started to heat up since they were focused on Calvin. That took some of the pressure off of me and I made the most of it. On one possession I made a three from the wing, forcing the Marion team to come out and guard me.

On another possession, when we were up two points, I cut toward the free-throw line and Brendan passed me the ball. When the Marion player came at me, I drove past him and made a lay-up. On our last possession, with five seconds left in the first half, Calvin shot a three, but he missed. I got the rebound and scored right before the buzzer sounded.

We had a four-point lead at halftime and after I made the shot to end the quarter, everyone was pumped up and ready for the second half.

Before the half started, Hal pulled me aside and told me to start looking for Willard and Calvin on the three-point line since Marion was leaving them wide open.

CHAPTER TWENTY-THREE
WILLARD'S BIG HALF

When the second half started, I began to look for Willard and sure enough he was open on almost every possession. He made the most of it. Willard scored twelve of his fifteen points in the third quarter. He helped us pull away from the Marion team.

When Willard started scoring, they started covering him, but that left Calvin open. Whenever Calvin was open, Brendan and me started passing the ball to him and he started scoring. Calvin would also end up with fifteen points after he made a couple of threes and two flagrant foul free throws after he took a major hit from one of Marion's biggest guys. Leading by four at halftime, we would pull away and ended up having a twelve-point lead going into the fourth quarter—things would only get worse for the Marion team.

In the fourth quarter we continued to pull away and Marion County guard ended up fouling out—when he went out, we knew we had won. With the point guard out, we packed our defense on the inside and we dared them to shoot it from the outside. This worked out perfectly.

We only gave up four points in the fourth quarter and ended up winning 54–36. I ended up with sixteen points while Calvin and Willard both scored fifteen. Brendan and Buckel had four points each, so nearly everyone got to score.

With the win we improved to 10-1 on the season and we were on an eight game winning stream. With the State Championship a couple of weeks away, we were feeling good about ourselves.

CHAPTER TWENTY-FOUR
GETTING HEALTHY AGAIN

Next week at practice we got some good news. First, we would have two final games before the State Championship started. We would play Damar on March 14th. We would then, two days later, play Boone County at Triton to finish the regular season. We were really excited because those two games were against teams we knew really well.

On top of that good news, we learned from Hal that both Cody and Sam were healthy. They would play both tomorrow and Saturday. We were glad to hear that since Calvin was on vacation with his family and wouldn't be back until next week. We needed Sam and Cody.

The next day we went up to Damar and got ready for our game with them and while we were warming up, I looked over at their team. I didn't think we were going to have much trouble with them.

Sure enough, we ended up winning 37-17. It was our best defensive performance of the season. We boxed out. We challenged their shooters. We forced them to turn the ball over a lot.

Both Cody and Sam played a lot of minutes to get them back to what they were before getting injured. Cody struggled with his shot from the deep, but his defense and decision making were still great.

Chris and Brendan both played great games. Chris dominated the boards on offense and scored a lot. Brendan drove to the basket and got layup after layup.

The only problem we did have was at the end of the game, Willard was showing off to the crowd and didn't shake hands with Damar after the game. Me and my teammates talked to him in the locker room. We told him that if he ever did that again, he would not play with us. He apologized and we left.

CHAPTER TWENTY-FIVE
BOONE COMES TO TOWN

March 16th, two days after beating Damar, our old friends Boone County came to Triton High School to play us for our final game of the regular season.

Since we had beat Damar, we had improved to 11-1 on the season and we were on a nine game winning streak. We were coming into this game with a lot of confidence even though Calvin wasn't with us.

This game was important to both me and Chris Vanarsdall since we were playing at Triton. Chris wanted to play well since he goes to school there and he kept saying that Triton was "his gym."

It was important to me because most of my friends and family were going to be there. I still felt bad for losing to Grant at the Arnie Tournament when they were there—I wanted to make it up to them.

After getting dressed in the locker room I went out to the court and sure enough they were all there: my mom, aunt Rita, Rosemary, Colin, Erin, Rooney, Michella, her son Matty, and my friends Sawyer, Garrett, Alex, Matthew, Brooklyn and Hayden. I had a big fan club and I was grateful for it. I was going to need their support.

When the game started, both teams got off to a very slow start on offense. I scored the first basket and got fouled. I missed the free-throw, so we only had a two-point lead.

Boone would take the lead briefly when they scored the next four points, but on our next possession, I shot the ball and missed; Chris Vanarsdall got the rebound and scored.

Later, Cody would drive by Boone's Chris Thompson and get to the basket, making a layup which gave us the lead again. For the rest of the game Boone would play catch up.

As the quarter went on, both teams' defenses would dominate as both teams would only score two points the rest of the way. Going into the second quarter we would lead Boone 8-6.

CHAPTER TWENTY-SIX
CHRIS VANARSDALL'S BIG QUARTER

While we were on the bench getting ready for the second quarter, Hal and Joe Pugh, a friend of ours who was helping Hal coach the game, decided to make a few changes.

On defense, they told us that we were going to play a 2-3 zone for the rest of the game. On offense, they said to attack the paint, to stop shooting from the outside so much.

When the quarter started, that's exactly what we did. On offense we started attacking the inside. My teammates were feeding me the ball in the post, but every time I got it, I was double teamed. Chris

Vanarsdall would get open every time when I was in trouble and he would score every time. He would end up scoring twelve points in the quarter and at the end of the game he would finish with sixteen to lead everyone.

While Chris Vanarsdall carried us on offense, our defense shut Boone down allowing us to pull away. Boone was beating us on the boards but for some reason they had a hard time scoring.

They had a lot of open looks but kept missing. On offense, Chris Vanarsdall kept getting open and scoring. This made Boone get more desperate and they made some bad decisions.

On one possession, Ryan Beard tried to shoot over me, but I blocked him and got the ball. I ran the other way and scored on a layup extending our lead.

On another possession, Horton tried to drive past me but lost control of the ball and it went out of bounds. We would score again, forcing Boone to take a timeout.

After the timeout, Boone's Chris Thompson got more aggressive, attacking the paint, somehow getting past me and Chris Vanarsdall, scoring which cut into our lead.

When we got to halftime we still had a pretty big lead, 24-11. Chris Vanarsdall had half of our points. He was playing a great game and the reason we were ahead.

CHAPTER TWENTY-SEVEN
BYE-BYE BOONE

When the second half started, Boone kept playing their zone defense so we just kept the ball on the outside, running the weave forcing them to come out and guard us.

When they did, we found open shots in their zone and we took advantage of it, scoring multiple times. When the third quarter ended we had a fourteen-point lead.

When the fourth quarter started, we got sloppy. Boone came right at us, not settling for jump shots like they were before, going into the paint and getting fouled.

Halfway through the quarter, our lead had been

cut to eight points. That's when we all stepped up as we always did when we were challenged.

After Chris Thompson made the free throws, cutting our lead to eight, I told Cody to get the ball to me on our next possession. It was time for me to step up.

I got the ball on the right wing and Horton and Richie, Boone's center, thought I was going to pass it again since that's all I was doing the entire quarter. When they didn't come out to guard me, I shot it and made it. This gave us a ten-point lead and Boone never seriously challenged us again for the rest of the game.

They didn't score and they started to foul us when the time started running out. They fouled Brendan a few times and he made most of his free throws, as did Sam and Cody when they were fouled.

The final score would be Shelby 40 and Boone 27. Chris Vanarsdall led all scorers with sixteen points, playing the best game of the season up to that point. We were all proud of him.

After the game, I talked to my friends and family, telling them thanks for coming and that I loved them. Later that evening, Cody, Kendra, Brandon, Cody's brother, his wife Ashley, and their two sons, and me went out for pizza to celebrate, not knowing that our toughest challenge was still ahead of us.

CHAPTER TWENTY-EIGHT
PREPARING FOR STATE

The Tuesday after we beat Boone, we found out who all was in our State Championship bracket. We also found out who we were playing and we knew that winning the Championship would not be easy.

First, Boone and Warrick would play each other with the winner of that game going on to play Grant. Nearly everyone on my team figured Warrick would have no trouble with Boone.

After those two games were finished my team would take on the Lake County Lakers, a team that we were familiar with and knew we could beat if we played a solid game. When I heard we were playing Lake County, I got scared because I knew who was on that team and I had never forgotten what had happened the last time that I faced him.

It was my rookie year, the 2008-2009 season at the Arnie Petre Tournament when I first played Lake County. They had a center, the same center that we would play, that dominated the game. He ended up scoring twenty-two points and had fifteen rebounds. We lost that game by well over twenty points that day. I also took the worst beating of my life in that game—with a twisted ankle, a bruised shoulder, and a sprained wrist.

After that game I told myself that if I ever played him and Lake County again, I would be ready. For the next ten years, I readied myself for the physical game I knew they would play. This time I would win.

That Wednesday, we had our final practice. Everyone was there and ready to go. Since it was our final practice, Hal and Joe Pugh had something special planned for us.

We were to scrimmage with some high school players, Joe's nephew, Dylan, and my friends Matthew and Carl, to help us get ready for the State Tournament that coming weekend. I was really pumped up for this scrimmage, not just because I wanted to get ready for State, but also because Zach Kuhn, Shelbyville star player, was there and I wanted to see how I could do against him.

We didn't keep score, but I'm sure we lost by over twenty points. We still had fun and I got to play against Zach, so I was happy. He was as good as everyone had said—playing against these six guys gave us confidence that would help us in the tournament. It was time for the real game to begin.

CHAPTER TWENTY-NINE
BRING ON LAKE COUNTY

On March 23rd we traveled to Ben Davis High School where the State Championship would take place. This is where all of our hard work this season would lead—hopefully to a Championship.

We arrived there that morning to watch Boone and Warrick play each other and sure enough, Warrick didn't have much trouble beating Boone, something we all expected.

After that game, we all went out and had lunch. After we were finished, we went back to Ben Davis to watch the Warrick and Grant game. We would play after them.

The Warrick and Grant game was intense, with

both teams having a lot of players foul out. When the fourth quarter started, Grant had so many players fouled out, they only had four players left to play. Warrick ended up beating them, so if we beat Lake County, we would play Warrick in the State Championship. After they were done playing we went onto the court and started warming up, preparing for the physical game to come.

When the game started, both teams came out swinging as hard as they could. Both me and the Lake County center would score the six first points in the quarter. The refs were calling the game tight on both teams, especially on travel calls. Every time Chris Vanarsdall did his pump fake and started dribbling, he was called for traveling.

We were also having trouble boxing out their big man on defense—he was getting offensive rebound after offensive rebound. We knew we had to make a change going into the second quarter.

When the first quarter ended, Lake County was up 10-8. Hal and Joe Pugh sat us down and told everyone to just relax, play together like we had all season. They also said that we were going to play a 3-2 zone on defense to see if it would slow Lake County down, especially on the boards. We went back out and the second quarter started.

In the second quarter, my teammates and I played more relaxed and in no time at all we retook the lead from Lake County. Our shots were starting to go in the basket.

On one possession I got the ball at the top of the key. I shot it and made it, giving us a three-point lead. On another possession, when Lake County started to full court press us, I set a screen on Cody's guy and Cody blew past him. He ended up making a ten-foot jumper, extending our lead.

On defense, our 3-2 zone was working. Lake County's center only got one offensive rebound. When he tried to shoot it, Cody came from behind and blocked him. Halfway through the quarter, when one of the Lake County guards tried to throw the ball inside, Chris Vanarsdall stole the ball and got it to Brendan who took it the other way and scored.

When the second quarter ended, we were up five points and feeling pretty confident about our chances, but in the second half, Lake County would come at us much harder.

In the third quarter, both teams' offenses couldn't score. Both defenses would challenge every shot and force a lot of turnovers because of the pressure both sides were putting on the ball handlers. Lake County continued to play full court man-to-man pressure on our guards. This resulted in both Brendan and Cody having trouble bring the ball down the court.

Our defense completely took over the inside and the offensive rebounding away from Lake County, forcing them to settle for long jump shots. Since both teams' defenses were playing so well, neither team could pull away from each other. It remained a close game the entire quarter.

We made a mistake to give Lake County the momentum. With ten seconds left in the quarter, we were up three points 21-18. Lake County shot a three from the baseline, but I blocked it and it went out of bounds with three seconds left.

Lake County got the ball out of bounds—they threw it in and shot another three and it missed, but Cody got called for a foul. Lake County got to shoot three free-throws.

They made all three, tying the game at twenty-one points each. We went to our bench where Hal and Joe gave us more instructions, because we all knew this game was going down to the wire.

CHAPTER THIRTY
A MAGICAL COMEBACK

When the fourth quarter started, we scored the first basket when Calvin cut backdoor on his defender and Brendan passed him the ball. Calvin made the ten-foot jump shot on the baseline.

On our next possession, I got the ball and drove it in on Lake's center. I took the shot and made it. I also got fouled, so I got to shoot one free throw. I made the free throw, so we had a five-point lead with three minutes to go, but then Lake came back at us with a big run of their own.

For the next two and a half minutes, we would not score while Lake would go on a 10-0 run to take a five-point lead with 30 seconds to go in the game.

After we missed another shot, Lake got the rebound and Chris Vanarsdall instantly committed a foul to stop the clock, sending Lake County to the free throw line.

When the Lake County player got up he said something to Chris and the referee heard it and he ended up giving the Lake County player a technical foul.

Lake County shot their 1-1 free throws. After they shot theirs, we would shoot our two technical foul free throws. They made their first free throw but missed their second, giving them a six-point lead, 32-26, with 30 seconds to go. It was time for us to go on our own magical run.

Hal Picked me to shoot the technical foul free throws. I went to the free throw line to shoot them and I made them both, cutting Lake County's lead to only four points. Since Lake got a technical foul against them, we got the ball again. On our next possession, Chris Vanarsdall passed the ball to Cody at half court.

I cut up to the top of the key and Cody passed me the ball. I thought about shooting the three, but Lake's center ran toward me. I went by him and shot a ten-foot jump shot in the paint. It bounced around the rim a couple of times, but it went in. Lake led 32-30 with fifteen seconds left in the game.

Lake inbounded the ball to their big man and we

tried to get the ball from him, but we couldn't. Sam fouled him, sending him to the free throw line with ten seconds left in the game.

CHAPTER THIRTY-ONE
THE SHOT

The Lake County center went to the free throw line to shoot the 1-1 and when he was getting ready to shoot I told myself *he has to be tired, he's played the entire game against me, so he is going to miss one of these free throws.*

Sure enough, he shot the first free throw and missed. I got the rebound and Hal immediately called a timeout to set up our final play.

We got in a huddle and both Joe Pugh and Hal told us to take what the defense gave us. They told us to not force anything because there was still 10 seconds left which was plenty of time to go down the court and get a good shot.

I told my teammates, "just get me the ball and I'll

win it." We went back out to the court and got ready to run the play that would determine our season.

Chris Vanarsdall inbounded the ball to Cody. When he got trapped, he passed it to Brendan who got it across half court on the right side. He cut left and got the ball back to Cody. Cody drove down the left wing but Cody got cut off, so he passed it to me at the free throw line. I took one dribble backwards to get behind the three-point line and I shot it with one second left on the clock.

As soon as the buzzer went off, the shot went in and the gym exploded. Before I knew it, my teammates were all around me, hugging me, but I was watching the refs since they were talking to each other in a huddle.

When my teammates saw who I was looking at, they starting looking at the refs too, as did the entire gymnasium. After what seemed like an eternity, the refs held their hands up, signaling it was a three-point shot and then the gym exploded again. We had won the game 33-32.

Cody tackled me to the ground and my teammates started piling up on me one by one. I remember telling them, with a big smile on my face, that I couldn't breathe. Eventually they all got off of me, but we all had big smiles on our faces and at that moment, it was the happiest I'd ever seen them.

After the game, so many people came up to me

and hugged me or said, "Great shot John!" Like the McQueary family, Stephanie and Lonnie, Cody's parents, and Ashley and Brandon, his brother and sister. Also Ryan Franklin, a good friend of mine and Kat Muth, a very close friend of mine and someone I liked a lot. After I got free from everyone, she came down and gave me a big hug and that was the happiest I've ever been.

Unfortunately, after that, Lake started saying stuff to Cody's family, so we had to break them up before they got in a fight.

We got everyone to the locker room and fortunately, Cody and his family calmed down. Hal reported Lake to the officials so they were escorted out and we could now focus on tomorrow.

CHAPTER THIRTY-TWO
THE CHAMPIONSHIP GAME

March 24, 2019, the day of the Championship—everything we went through this season, the good and the bad, helped us to get to this day. I just had a feeling that we were going to pull this out.

That morning, Hal picked me up and we went to Coulston to shoot around in the gym and to meet the rest of the team there. We shot around there for about an hour. I talked to Cody while we were there to make sure he was okay. He told me he was and his family would be there cheering for us. We went to the school and when we got there I got a pleasant surprise. Brian and Tammy Gumberts were there along with Jake Gumberts and Sue, along with Alex

Jones and my cousin Michella and her husband Tony and son Matty. Susan, Todd and Shane Hill were there along with Ashley Hankins, Abby Shuck, Jonah Thacker, and Mike and Theresa Vanarsdall. The McQueary's were also there. When I saw all of them, I felt a lot better since I was really nervous. They would give me the support I needed. I waved to them and then me and my teammates started to warm up.

During warmups the refs pulled me and the captain from the Warrick team to half court. They told us they wanted us to play a good clean game and not to cause any trouble because there would be consequences. Me and the Warrick captain shook hands and we went back to our teams. I told my teammates what the refs had said, but I knew that we would play clean, so I wasn't too worried about it.

We continued to warm up and as we did, more and more of our friends came in to the gym, like Susan, Todd and Shane, along with Abby, one of the coaches from another Shelby County team, and Ashley our County Coordinator.

The buzzer sounded, so we went to our bench and got ready to play for the championship. First Hal and Joe gave us some last minute instructions.

They told us to relax and play hard, not to get nervous, and come out with a good start—that we already had beat this team once, so we could do it again. We put our hands together and yelled "Magic!" and got ready to play.

CHAPTER THIRTY-THREE
A PHYSICAL FIRST HALF

Before the game started, they introduced the starting line-ups for both teams. Ours was the same as it was when we were all healthy: me, Calvin, Cody, Brendan, and Chris, with Sam, Willard, and Buckel coming off the bench. We shook hands with Warrick and wished them good luck and congratulated them for making it this far. We then headed to center court to tip-off and get the game started.

When we tipped off, I tipped it forward to Calvin, but he didn't have an advantage so he passed it to Cody who got our offense set up.

Warrick came out playing a man-to-man defense,

so I went down to the block and posted my man up. When Cody passed me the ball I went right to work, going straight to the basket and scoring to give us an early lead.

When we went on defense, we came out in a 3-2 zone. That confused Warrick since we always played a 1-3-1 zone and that's what they were planning for. Thanks to our defense, we managed to pull away early, forcing Warrick to play catch up the entire game.

As the first quarter went on, our lead grew and as Warrick became more frustrated they got more physical. On one play I got the ball and before I could get a shot off, I got hit and fell to the floor.

The ref called a foul and after that Cody came up to me and said, "John, don't wait for the hit to come, shoot it as soon as it comes to you and you will get to the free-throw line."

On our next possession, after Warrick scored, cutting our lead to six, I did what Cody said and sure enough I got hit again as I shot the ball and the ref called another foul.

I made the shot but missed the free throw. We still had an eight-point lead at the end of the first quarter, but things would get harder for us in the second.

In the second quarter, neither team scored very much. Warrick had trouble penetrating our zone so they settled for outside shots but didn't make many of them. They also couldn't get many rebounds because Chris Vanarsdall kept getting them.

Chris Vanarsdall would lead everyone with fourteen rebounds and his defense was a big reason why Warrick had trouble scoring in the paint.

When we were on offense, I was getting double teamed. I had to pass the ball back out and for some reason, no one on the team could score.

Yeah, Cody missed a couple of threes at the top of the key. Brendan had trouble penetrating into the paint, something he liked to do as he had trouble shooting from the outside.

Chris Vanarsdall was covered tight on the inside so we couldn't get the ball to him, but fortunately Calvin managed to cut backdoor when I was doubled, so we got the ball to him and he scored.

Midway through the quarter, I drove to the basket but got cut off. Buckel snuck behind the defense so I passed the ball to him and he shot it but got fouled. As he got ready to shoot the free throws, me and Chris looked at each other and nodded, knowing Buckel wasn't a good foul shooter and to get ready for the rebound, yet somehow Buckel made both, extending our lead to ten points again.

A couple of minutes later, I missed a shot and Warrick got the rebound. They started to push it down the court and for some reason they shot a three and it missed.

I grabbed the rebound, but when I got the ball I caught someone's elbow to my face while I was still in the air as I had jumped to get the rebound. The back of my head hit the floor hard.

Instantly the refs stopped play and both teams went to their benches while Hal and Joe came over to check on me. After a couple of minutes, I got back on my feet and headed to the bench where I got tested to see if I had a concussion, but fortunately the doctor said I was fine, so I went back in the game.

CHAPTER THIRTY-FOUR
THE FINAL HALF

When halftime started, we were up ten points and feeling good about ourselves. Hal and Joe reminded us that there was still one half left to go, so we had to stay aggressive.

The third quarter started and it went pretty much how the first half did, with both defenses making it hard for the other team to score. That's when we decided to run.

After Warrick shot another three, I got the rebound and passed the ball to Cody. I sprinted down the court beating my guy when Cody passed it back to me and I scored on a layup.

After a couple of possessions, when we had an

eight-point lead, one of the Warrick players drove down the lane and tried to shoot over me, but I blocked his shot. Calvin got the ball and drove down the court, scoring, and extended our lead to ten again. With a minute left in the quarter, Brendan finally scored on a ten-foot jumper to give us a twelve-point lead. That would be the final points either team would score that quarter.

Going into the fourth quarter up twelve points, we figured that we had the game under control, but then Warrick came at us full force as soon as the quarter started.

One minute into the quarter, Warrick hit two three-point shots to cut our lead in half, but on our next possession, Brendan got the ball to Calvin and Calvin made a three on the baseline to extend our lead to nine points.

Warrick made another on their next possession. When we got the ball back, we got it to Calvin who made yet another three to get our lead back up. We wouldn't score again until the final minute and Warrick would get within three points.

For the next three minutes, when we were on offense, we would turn the ball over, take bad shots, or just not run our offense like we had the first three quarters. It also didn't help when Chris Vanarsdall and a Warrick player got double technical fouls and Hal decided to sit Chris Vanarsdall down for a couple of minutes.

With thirty seconds left in the game, we were up three points after Cody made one of two free throws. Warrick came down the court and they shot a three to tie it.

It hit the front of the rim and bounced out. I grabbed the rebound and Warrick instantly fouled me. I went to the free-throw line to shoot to 1-1. I got to the free throw line knowing I was about to shoot the biggest free throws of the game and the season. I shot the first one and made it. I shot the second and made it too, giving us a five-point lead.

Warrick went down the court and with ten seconds left they shot a long three that also missed. I got the rebound and I got the ball to Cody who was fouled.

Cody went to the free throw line and again he would make one of two free throws to give us a six-point lead. Warrick took one long three and they missed again. Chris Vanarsdall grabbed the rebound and the buzzer sounded. The game was over, we won. The final score was Magic 32 Warrick 26. We were THE STATE CHAMPIONS!

CHAPTER THIRTY-FIVE
STATE CHAMPIONS!!!

As soon as the buzzer sounded, we started celebrating. Hugging each other and yelling "State Champs!". We shook hands with Warrick and told them good game. Then we got our medals.

After we had our medals, I stayed in the gym along with most of my teammates. I talked to all of my friends and family who came. I thanked all of them.

I took pictures with them and my teammates. We all went to the locker room to change out of our uniforms for the last time and we all said goodbye to each other, thanking each other for a great season. Then we all had to go home.

When I got home, Hal dropped me off and said "Good season John, you were good this year."

I replied, "Thanks, I will see you again soon." I went inside my house and my mom was there waiting.

I told her how the game had gone and she congratulated me and I thanked her. I went to my room and hung up my medal. I laid in my bed and kept thinking about the past two days.

Later that night, I went to the Langkabel's house and they threw me a small party with a few banners that said "Johnny" and "State Champion" on them. I thanked them and told them that I really appreciated it.

Two weeks later our season would officially come to an end when we had our celebration dinner at Cagney's Pizza King where I stuffed up on pizza and tacos.

Hal gave us a speech saying he was proud of us this season and we were the best Magic team he'd ever coached. We all told him that he was the best coach that we could ask for.

As the evening went on, Chris Vanarsdall said that Triton had hired a new basketball coach and he was going to try out for them again, so he might not be there for the next season.

Sam also said he was retiring from the Magic and that he would play for Joe Land's team next season.

We wished them both luck and thanked them for all they did for us this season and that we would miss them.

We all went home and as soon as I got home, I started preparing for next season since we had a title to defend.

That's how our season went and everything we had to go through to win a championship. I hope that you've enjoyed reading this story as much as I had writing it. Thank you for all the support you gave us and hopefully I'll see you supporting us next season. GO MAGIC!

The End

ACKNOWLEDGEMENTS

    This last section is for my teammates, coaches, friends, and family. I appreciate everything you all have done for me—you all helped me become the player and person I am today.

    You all are the reason why this season was a magical one. That's why I wanted to write about it, because I never want to forget it again. Thank you all for the support you gave us and I can't wait to see you all again next season. GO MAGIC!!!

MY THANKS TO SPECIAL OLYMPICS

I want to dedicate these pages to all my coaches and teammates who made this season as great as it was. I've been playing for the Magic for eleven years now, but this season was by far my favorite.

Not just because we won the State Championship but because we had SO much fun and because of all of the support we received from our fans and close friends.

Like Joe Land, helping during our practices, especially banging up on me to get me ready for our games.

Joe Pugh, who helped us during our practices and helped Hal out with coaching a few of our games including our State Championship.

Abby Shuck and Ashley Hankins, two of our biggest fans who supported us a lot during our State Championship games. Thanks to them for everything they have done.

SHOUTOUT TO MY TEAMMATES

To my teammates for making this season as great as it was, I want to dedicate this to them for all of their hard work and how they stepped up during the season to win a State Championship. I am really lucky to have you guys as teammates.

First, our rookie Willard Sapp. When we first met him he proved right away that he could score. He is a great outside shooter and knows how to get to the rim and finish. I was most proud of him when Cody and Sam went down with injuries and he was put into the starting lineup against Grant and Marion County. If he didn't play the way he did in those two games, we probably wouldn't have won.

Next, our forward, Chris Vanarsdall. He improved so much this season—if he keeps improving the way he did, the skies the limit for him. When the season started, he was rusty, not scoring or rebounding well, but after our Arnie Petre Tradition Tournament, he started to improve and become one of our top players. During the Wabash, Taylor, and State tournaments, Chris was one of our top scorers and rebounders. I was really proud of how he stepped up and contributed to the team after a rough start.

Next we have John Buckel who has been on our team for a few years now. In my opinion last season was probably his best season. Again, when injuries struck, Buckel saw more playing time and, like Willard, Buckel stepped up and contributed when we needed him to. His defense against Grant County when we played them at Taylor was a big reason why we beat them. During the State Championship game, Buckel hit two big free throws to help us stay ahead. I was proud of how he stepped up too.

Now we have Calvin Hanna, one of our starting guards. Calvin has been on the Magic for a long time and he's always been one of our top offensive players. Last season was no different, as time and time again, Calvin came up big in clutch-situations such as the Seymour tournament, it was Calvin who hit the free throws to ice the game against Warrick County. He also hit the three point shot against Grant to put us up nine points with 15 seconds left in game. In the fourth quarter of the State Championship game against Warrick, Calvin hit two big three pointers when Warrick was making their comeback—those two three-pointers helped us stay ahead and eventually win the game.

There is also Sam Gambrel, the son of our head coach, Hal Gambrel. Sam has been on the team longer than anyone else and he is one of our vocal leaders. His leadership and commitment to help the team win is another big reason why this team has been so successful these past few years. Sam is someone I have a lot of respect for and someone I am proud to call a teammate.

Then there is Brendan Harris—another one of our starting guards. Brendan is the most athletic player on the team and he is probably our best defender.

When he is on the court, our defense goes to another level. He is a great ball handler and does a great job attacking the basket and finishing. He has been on the team for a few years now and ever since he joined, the Magic has been very tough to beat.

My last teammate is our starting point guard and my best friend, Cody McQueary. Cody is probably our best two-way player. On offense he can shoot the three and he's also great at making decisions on where to pass the ball and he knows how to beat defenses. On defense he is very vocal, a great rebounder, and great at anticipating passes and stealing the ball. The Magic wouldn't be as good if Cody wasn't on the team—we are very thankful to have him.

I am very happy and glad to have them playing with me on the Magic and hopefully we can continue to play with each other for many more years to come.

Lastly, to my Coach, Hal Gambrel, who has been the best coach I could ever ask for. A great coach and a great friend, someone I really look up to. Words can't even explain how much I appreciate and respect him. Again, thanks for everything Hal.

TO MY FAMILY

I want to dedicate this final piece to my family for all of the support they've given me. I wouldn't be the player or person I am today if I didn't have them. When I got cut from the high school team, I felt like I let everyone down in my family. I couldn't even look my grandma in the eye when I told her.

Nearly everyone on my mom's side of the family had played high school basketball at some point in their lives and some of them even played college ball.

My uncle Richard was a great player for Morristown back in the 70s and he went to college at Hanover where he played for a year—he was also great at track and broke a few records at that time.

There are my cousins Michella and Erin Nigh. They played basketball for Morristown back in the early 2000s and they both would finish in the Top 5 in scoring when they played.

I was only in elementary school and junior high, but I still remember going to most of their games because back then they were my idols. I really looked up to them and I remember telling my mom that someday I was going to be as good as them. Like Uncle Richard, both Michella and Erin would go on to play college ball.

Michella would play at Hanover for a couple of years and Erin went on to Christian Brothers University in Tennessee and they both would have great careers. They also played volleyball for Morristown, winning numerous titles and my cousin Erin won the State Championship in 2003. They were both amazing athletes while they were at Morristown.

My grandpa, Norman Morris, was one of the most successful coaches in Morristown history. He spent nearly 25 years at Morristown as a teacher, coach, and athletic director; during that time, he won four section titles and five county championships. He also coached the girls team, winning two county championships with them and my mom, Ruth Ann, was the manager of those teams.

My aunts, Rita and Rosemary both played four years at Morristown, but unfortunately didn't win any county or sectional titles, but they were amazing athletes. Later on, Aunt Rosemary would coach at Morristown for a few years and had some success.

My aunt Gina and my mom didn't play much high school basketball but did do other things. My mom managed the girls team and my Aunt Gina played tennis and golf.

My grandma, Mary Morris, has always supported me and helped me believe in myself even when things got hard for me. I appreciate and respect her a lot.

My sister Jennifer, my brother David, and my mom were always there for me, supporting me. I love you guys and thank God that you guys are in my life.

I also want to thank the Langkabels, Kristi and Leigh—their children, Dylan, Hayden, and Brooklyn helped me get better by playing against me. Thanks to them for everything they have done for me.

TO THE MORRISTOWN COMMUNITY

Thank you to Morristown for all the support you gave to me and my teammates. I think that after the Jackets won the State Championship in 2018, it made us believe that we could win a championship too. Thanks to Morristown for setting the bar high for us.

2018-2019 Shelby County Magic

Regular Season:

January 5:	Clark County	47-24 W
January 5:	Warrick County	34-29 W
February 2:	Grant County	43-44 L
February 2:	Howard County	36-25 W
February 3:	Porter County	46-35 W
February 3:	Boone County	45-40 W
February 9:	Franklin County	50-22 W
February 11:	Marion County East	47-28 W
February 25:	Warren Gold	46-35 W
March 2:	Grant County	40-31 W
March 6:	Marion County	54-36 W
March 14:	Damar	37-17 W
March 16:	Boone County	40-27 W

State Championship:

March 23:	Lake County	33-32 W
March 24:	Warrick County	32-26 W

Made in the USA
Middletown, DE
12 December 2019